CULTURE
in Malaysia

Melanie Guile

Raintree

Chicago, Illinois

© 2005 Raintree
Published by Raintree,
A division of Reed Elsevier, Inc.

For information, address the publisher:
Raintree, 100 N. LaSalle, Suite 1200, Chicago, IL 60602

Customer Service: 888-363-4266
Visit our website at www.raintreelibrary.com

Printed in China by WKT Company Ltd.

09 08 07 06 05
10 9 8 7 6 5 4 3 2 1

Library of Congress Cataloging-in-Publication Data

Guile, Melanie.
Culture in Malaysia / Melanie Guile.-- 1st ed.
     p. cm. -- (Culture in--)
   Includes bibliographical references and index.
   ISBN 1-4109-1133-0 (hc, library binding)
   1. Malaysia--Civilization--Juvenile literature. I. Title. II. Series: Guile, Melanie. Culture in--
   DS594.G85 2004
   306'.09595--dc22
                                        2004016650

Acknowledgments
The publisher would like to thank the following for permission to reproduce photographs: AAP/AFP Photo/Ahmad Yusni: p. 10; AFP Photo/Ahmad Yusni: p. 9; © Asiaworksphotos.com/Munshi Ahmed: p. 16, /Mark Fallander: p. 27; Australian Picture Library/Corbis: pp. 12, 13, 14, 21; Bernard Chandran: p. 15 (lower); EMI Music Malaysia, for album cover: p. 20; Shirley Geok-lin Lim: p. 23; Great Southern Stock: p. 29; © Piers Cavendish/Impact Photos: p. 17; © Lonely Planet Images/Richard I'Anson: p. 28, /Mark Daffey: p. 6, /Chris Mellor: p. 15 (upper); Hikayat Sang Kanchil © OUP 1963: p. 22; Photolibrary.com: p. 19; The P Ramlee Cyber Museum, www.p-ramlee.com: p. 24; Reuters: pp. 7, 8; Travelcom Asia/Mike Reed: p. 11, /Wayne Tarman: pp. 18, 26; Vision New Media: p. 25.

Cover photograph of Malaysian folk dancers reproduced with permission of Photolibrary.com/James Montgomery.

Every effort has been made to contact copyright holders of any material reproduced in this book. Any omissions will be rectified in subsequent printings if notice is given to the publishers.

The paper used to print this book comes from sustainable resources.

CONTENTS

Culture in Malaysia   4

Traditions and Customs   8

Minority Groups   12

Costumes and Clothing   14

Food   16

Performing Arts   18

Folklore and Literature   22

Film and Television   24

Arts and Crafts   26

Glossary   30

Index   32

Some words are shown in bold, **like this.** You can find out what they mean by looking in the glossary.

CULTURE IN
Malaysia

The Malaysian Peninsula lies on the great trading routes between India and China—a gateway to the fabled Spice Islands of Indonesia. For centuries, waves of people came to trade and settle on its shores, joining the Malays and the **indigenous** tribal peoples, the *Orang Asli*. The Portuguese, the Dutch, and then the English invaded the country, setting up profitable rubber **plantations** and tin mines. Chinese and Indian immigrants also streamed in to share in the wealth.

Malaya achieved **independence,** or *Merdeka,* in 1957, and the states of Sarawak and Sabah were added in 1963 to form the Federation of Malaysia. Since then, the country has achieved great stability and prosperity through a strong government and hard work.

The Malaysian Peninsula—the mainland—is also called West Malaysia. East Malaysia, consisting of Sabah and Sarawak, lies across the South China Sea on a huge island called Borneo. Thirteen *negeri*, or states, and three federal territories make up the federation. Together with its islands, Malaysia is about the same size as New Mexico.

Most of the major cities are located on the Malaysian Peninsula, which is the most developed part of the country. This is also where Malaysia's nine sultans live. These traditional kings head the nine states in the western part of the country. Every five years one is elected king of Malaysia. The people of Sabah and Sarawak in the east mostly belong to **ethnic groups** and are different from the Malays in the western part of the country.

Flag of Malaysia

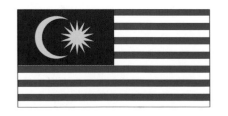

The national flag of Malaysia has fourteen red and white stripes that stand for its thirteen states, all equal under the one **federal** government. The gold star and crescent are traditional **Islamic** symbols and are shown in the Malaysian royal color to represent Malaysia's nine kings.

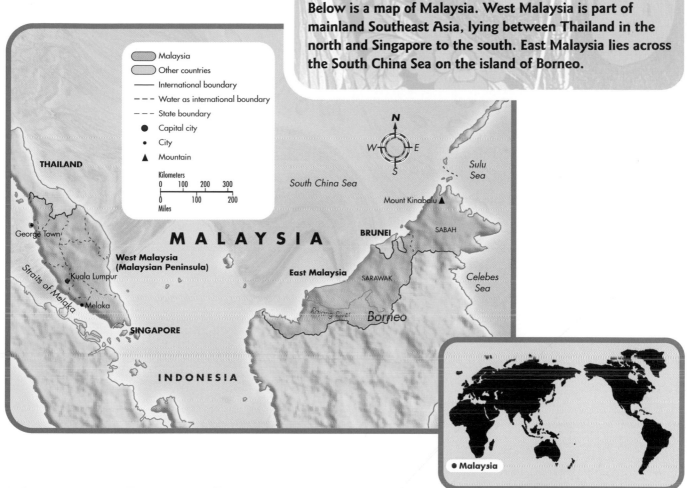

Below is a map of Malaysia. West Malaysia is part of mainland Southeast Asia, lying between Thailand in the north and Singapore to the south. East Malaysia lies across the South China Sea on the island of Borneo.

Map legend:

- Malaysia
- Other countries
- International boundary
- Water as international boundary
- State boundary
- ● Capital city
- • City
- ▲ Mountain

Kilometers
0   100   200   300
0   100   200
Miles

THAILAND

South China Sea

Sulu Sea

Mount Kinabalu ▲

George Town

MALAYSIA

BRUNEI

SABAH

West Malaysia (Malaysian Peninsula)

Kuala Lumpur

East Malaysia

SARAWAK

Celebes Sea

Straits of Melaka

Melaka

Rajang River

Borneo

SINGAPORE

INDONESIA

● Malaysia

What Is Culture?

Culture is a people's way of living. It is the way in which people identify themselves as a group, separate and different from any other. Culture includes a group's spoken and written language, social customs, and habits, as well as its traditions of art, crafts, dance, drama, music, literature, and religion.

Malaysians tend to define themselves by their ethnic group rather than their country. Communities live side-by-side but generally educate their children in their own language and keep their own religion, traditions, and values. While young people enjoy **censored** American television shows, rock bands, and fashions, Western values are discouraged. Former prime minister Mahathir Mohamad championed a community-based set of Asian values, which put the common good before personal freedom. His successor, Prime Minister Abdullah Ahmad Badawi, appears likely to continue this trend.

Strong Leadership

Dr. Mahathir Mohamad headed Malaysia's elected government from 1981 to 2003. He helped transform Malaysia into a modern industrial nation, with Kuala Lumpur as its thriving capital. Nevertheless, since 1998, unrest over government **corruption** has led to calls for *reformasi,* or reforms, including a reduction in the leader's power.

Ethnic Mix

Malaysia has a population of 23 million, which is made up of 58 percent Malays, 24 percent Chinese, 8 percent Indians, and about 5 percent **indigenous** people—the *Orang Asli*.

Although most Malays are farmers, they dominate in government, the military, and politics. Their language, *Bahasa Malaysia*, is the national language, although English is encouraged in higher education. Malaysian Chinese enjoy the highest standard of living of any **ethnic group.** They live mainly in cities, running businesses or working as doctors or lawyers. Peranakans, also known as Straits Chinese, are of mixed Malay-Chinese heritage. They have lived on the Malaysian Peninsula for 400 years and have developed their own language and culture and have a prosperous lifestyle.

This traditional longhouse in East Malaysia is home to many families belonging to the same tribal group.

The British brought many people from India to Malaysia in the late 1800s to work as laborers on rubber plantations. While middle-class Indians excel in medicine, law, and business, many others live in poverty on country **plantations** or in **shantytowns.** Recently, there has been a growing **racial tension** between poorer Indians and neighboring Malays.

A great variety of indigenous communities also live in traditional villages in remote forests, particularly in Sabah and Sarawak. *Orang Asli* and Malays are classed as *bumiputra*, or "sons of the soil."

Prayers are an essential part of life for Muslims. Formal prayers are observed before dawn, at noon, in the afternoon, at sunset, and in the evening.

Race Relations

Race riots in 1969 led to the New Economic Policy (NEP) in 1971, which favors *Orang Asli* and Malays in education, land, housing, and jobs. The NEP aims to reduce the wealth and power of the Chinese and ensure others a more equal share. Today, violence between ethnic groups is rare. Still, surveys indicate that only three percent of people mix socially with other ethnic groups, and political parties are based on race. Additionally, non–Malays increasingly oppose the NEP, claiming it is unfair. Despite these issues, ethnic **tolerance** is regarded as one of Malaysia's greatest achievements since **independence** in 1957.

Religions

There is great religious **diversity** in Malaysia, with **Muslim** Malays, **Christian** or **Hindu** Indians, **Buddhist** or Christian Chinese, and the ancient **animist** beliefs of the *Orang Asli*. Religious freedom is guaranteed under the country's **constitution.**

Islam

Islam is the official state religion, and about 52 percent of the population is Muslim. Islam has five basic laws for living a good life—faith in Allah (God), praying five times a day, giving to the poor, fasting during the holy month of Ramadan, and going on **pilgrimages** to Mecca. Malays are mostly of the moderate Sunni sect, and the government discourages the more extreme Shi'ah form. In the past twenty years, however, Shi'ah has spread in the north, and **Syariah Law** now applies to Muslims in the states of Kelantan and Terengganu. Many believe that Syariah Law is particularly harsh on women.

Nonyas and *Babas*

Over four centuries, Peranakans, or Straits Chinese, have developed a unique culture around the ancient trading port of Melaka. When wealthy Chinese merchants married local Malay women, these people soon developed their own language, customs, and tastes. Famous for their cooking, Peranakan wives, or *nonyas,* displayed their wealth in richly beaded and embroidered costumes. Their husbands, or *babas,* established lavishly furnished houses. Peranakans still take a leading role in public affairs.

TRADITIONS and Customs

In **multicultural** Malaysia, Indian **Hindu** festivals, Chinese **ancestor** worship, and tribal—or *Orang Asli*—**rituals** are all accepted and add to the richness of everyday life. But the dominant cultural influence is **Islam,** together with an undercurrent of traditional law called *adat.*

Adat—Malay Traditional Law

Adat is an ancient set of customs developed by Malay people for peaceful living. According to *adat*, community and family are more important than the individual. Politeness and cooperation called *gotong royong* are key values. Modest, quiet self-control is considered the best way to behave for both men and women. Those who do not follow these unwritten rules are considered selfish and rude.

Two Muslim women choose their *Hari Raya* greeting cards in downtown Kuala Lumpur.

Islamic Values

Religious duties are very important for **Muslim** Malays, and the rules governing dress and behavior are strictly observed. Both women and men attend **mosque** on Fridays but sit in different areas. Family life is highly valued, and the home is seen as a safe haven where the extended family can relax. Moderate Islam has a tradition of educating girls, which contributes to Malaysia's high literacy rate of 87 percent. Eleven years of free schooling is provided, although not all children attend.

Hari Raya Puasa

Hari Raya Puasa is the Islamic festival that celebrates the end of the fasting month of Ramadan. After 29 or 30 days of not eating or drinking between dawn and dusk, Muslims attend mosque, decorate their houses, put on their best clothes, and enjoy a family feast. It is a time for sharing and openness, and it is traditional for Muslims to travel home for this special celebration.

A shopping mall in Kuala Lumpur is decorated with lanterns for the Moon Cake Festival.

Malaysian Chinese Traditions

The extended family is very important in Chinese culture, and most households keep shrines to their ancestors. Duty and obedience to parents are expected, education is highly valued, and men make the key decisions affecting the family. The Chinese community places great emphasis on the rewards of hard work, and their festivals are an opportunity to celebrate the year's successes.

Chinese New Year

During Chinese New Year, usually in January or February depending on the **lunar** calendar, houses are cleaned and decorated with flowers; joss sticks, or incense; and candles. Families make offerings to their ancestors and pray at **Buddhist** temples. Children pay their respects to their parents and receive little red money envelopes called *ang pow.* Firecrackers, dragon dances, and street parades complete the celebrations.

Hungry Ghosts and Moon Cake Festivals

The Hungry Ghosts Festival in July or August is a time when the spirits of the dead are said to walk on Earth. Offerings of food are made, and paper money is burned to keep them happy and ensure good luck. The Moon Cake Festival is an ancient harvest celebration held in September. Decorated paper lanterns make a wonderful sight, and people gaze at the full moon and eat moon cakes made of bean paste, lotus seeds, and eggs.

Indian Malaysian Traditions

Most Indians in Malaysia are **Hindu** Tamils from South India, and their traditions remain strong. Women wear the graceful *sari*, boys are favored over girls because they take care of the family, and arranged marriages are accepted. Hindus worship hundreds of different gods and goddesses and believe in **reincarnation.** To avoid an endless cycle of rebirth, Hindus follow three paths to **salvation—devotion,** good deeds, and meditation. Weekly offerings of food and flowers are made to the gods and goddesses at temples, and most homes have a small altar to the family god where prayers are said. Hindus celebrate their festivals and holy days at temples and shrines.

Festival of Lights

The beautiful Festival of Lights called *Deepavali* in October or November celebrates the victory of good over evil in Hindu legend. In Indian areas, houses and streets are lit up, and **intricate** floor decorations are made with colored beans and rice grains. At this time of renewal, new clothes are worn and families gather to celebrate the occasion.

Colored grains are used to make intricate floor patterns at *Deepavali,* the Festival of Lights.

TRADITIONS *and Customs*

Thaipusam

The festival of *Thaipusam* in January or February is banned in India but survives in Hindu Tamil communities in Malaysia. Every year up to 100,000 people climb the steep steps to the temple inside the spectacular Batu Caves outside Kuala Lumpur. Men walk in procession carrying huge decorated cagelike structures called *kavad*. They are attached to their bodies by hooks and needles stuck into their bare flesh. The men work themselves into a **trance** through prayer and fasting, so that their wounds do not bleed. As they reach the shrine of Lord Muruga, the *kavadi* are removed, signalling the lifting of the burden of sins.

Gawai Dayak

Sarawak's main holiday is *Gawai Dayak*, a rice harvest festival celebrated by **indigenous** people in May and June. Among the Iban people, the spirit of greed is cast out at *Gawai* to rid the village of bad luck. First, the sacred carving of the hornbill bird is decorated with flowers, feathers, and beads. Then two boys drag a basket through the central corridor of the large **communal** hut called the longhouse, and families throw goods into it for the greedy spirit. Next, a bird is killed as a **sacrifice** to the hornbill spirit, while the people feast on sugar rice cakes called *penganan* and rice wine called *tuak*. The following day is an open house called *ngabang,* when friends and strangers are welcomed with more eating and celebrating.

National Holidays

In **multicultural** Malaysia, the main public holidays highlight the values and events to which all citizens can relate:

- Labor Day, on May 1, acknowledges the contribution of workers around the world.
- King's Birthday, on the first Saturday in June, celebrates the role of the **monarchy** in preserving Malaysia's traditions and customs.
- **Independence** Day, on August 31, celebrates the day when the country became an independent nation, free from foreign rule.

Villagers celebrate the rice harvest festival of *Gawai Dayak* with rituals to honor the sacred hornbill spirit.

MINORITY GROUPS

Before the Malays, Chinese, and Indians arrived, **indigenous** tribes lived in the forests of Malaysia. Some farmed the land, but most were **nomads** who killed their prey with poisoned blowpipes and fished in the rivers.

Throughout Malaysia, these indigenous tribes are known as *Orang Asli*, or original people. Because they are generally disadvantaged compared with other **ethnic groups,** the government **designates** them *bumiputras*, or "sons of the soil" and gives them special privileges in housing, education, and jobs. Many *Orang Asli* still live in remote areas of the Malay peninsula and Sabah and Sarawak, maintaining their unique cultures.

Northern Borneo

Northern Borneo is almost entirely undeveloped, and the indigenous tribes there make up about 50 percent of the population.

The Iban

The largest ethnic group in Sarawak are the Iban, who number about 450,000. Once feared headhunters and pirates, the Iban now live in extended families in longhouses along the major rivers. Traditionally **animists** who believed that spirits inhabit all things, the Iban worshiped the hornbill bird. Although many have now converted to **Christianity,** the rice harvest ceremony called *Gawai* still honors the bird spirit, whose wooden image is worshiped with chants, dances, and offerings.

The Kadazans retain many of their spirit-worship, or animist, traditions. Their distinctive black costumes are worn on special occasions.

The Kadazans

The Kadazans of Sabah are inland farmers who celebrate the rice harvest called *Pesta Kaamatan* every May. The Rice Spirit *Bambaazon* —is called home by a priestess— the *Bobohizan*—who uses an ancient language for her chants, with much celebrating.

The Bajau

The Bajau are rice farmers who live on the coast of Sabah. Originally called sea gypsies because they roamed the seas for fishing grounds, today the Bajau are best known as the "cowboys of the East" for their brilliant horse-riding skills. The Bajau also raise buffalo, which are an important form of wealth in their communities.

Malaysian Peninsula

In the more developed Malaysian Peninsula, indigenous peoples now make up less than one percent of the population.

Cultures Under Threat

Some groups of *Orang Asli* still inhabit the forests, growing their crops in burned-out clearings before moving on. But dam builders, miners, and logging companies have forced many communities off their lands and destroyed the forests on which they depend. The government is also putting pressure on nomadic *Orang Asli* to settle in villages, claiming their traditional farming methods harm the environment. Despite international protests, the government has so far refused to grant land ownership to any *Orang Asli* peoples.

The Temiars

The Temiars are farmers who live in longhouses in the northern hills. Well known for their nonviolence, the Temiars base their beliefs on dreams, which are seen as glimpses into the spirit world. Prayers, music, and dancing call up the protective spirit called *gunig,* who communicates through a shaman, or priest. The Temiars are taught to hurt no living thing, and people around the world have copied their dream **rituals,** trying to achieve the same peaceful way of life.

The Jahai

The Jahai are hunter-gatherers who do not live on settled farms but build temporary shelters in the forest while hunting with blowpipes and gathering fruits and herbs. They also rely on the forest for **rattan** and bamboo to build huts and weave mats. Government policies to settle them in permanent villages and log their traditional lands are a threat to the ancient Jahai culture.

The Jahai still live and hunt in remote jungles on the Malaysian Peninsula.

COSTUMES
and Clothing

There is a strong government push in Malaysia to encourage traditional Malay clothes over Western-style clothing, such as business suits and skirts. This sometimes unsettles Indian and Chinese Malaysians, who usually prefer Western clothing for everyday wear. In 2003 the issue came to a head when eight non-Malay politicians refused to wear traditional Malay dress as a "uniform." The order was not upheld, but clothing can still be a sensitive issue in **multicultural** Malaysia.

An Iban woman wears traditional dress.

Indigenous Clothing

The **indigenous** *Orang Asli* have ancient traditions of weaving, dying, and sewing their own costumes. The Iban women of Sarawak weave glowing colors into their highly decorated tops, which are trimmed with pompoms, beads, and silver. Long, straight sarong skirts are worn with belts decorated with silver coins, and hand-beaten silver armbands are worn as jewelry. The Bajau of Sabah are famous for their elaborate wedding costumes of yellow silk—the color of royalty—with brightly colored embroidered panels. The bride also wears a boat-shaped silver headpiece called a *sarempak* decorated with dangling silver ornaments. Traditional costumes like these are worn only for special ceremonies, and Western-style casual clothes are worn by most *Orang Asli*.

Traditional Clothing

The *baju melayu* is the traditional Malay men's costume and is still widely worn, especially to Friday mosque. A long-sleeved shirt is worn over loose pants called *seluar* and teamed with a brimless cap called a *songkok*. Twenty years ago, women usually wore the *baju kebaya*, a blouse and slim sarong skirt, but today most wear the *baju kurung*. The loose-fitting long top, matching long skirt, and headscarf called a *tudung* are designed to hide all but the woman's face and hands. Fabrics are usually **batik** or colorful prints and florals. *Baju kurung* is worn as a uniform in Islamic girls' schools.

A group of young boys attend mosque in Melaka wearing traditional men's costumes.

Fashion Design

After a slow start, Malaysian fashion has taken off, and designers now showcase their clothes at government-sponsored fashion events in Kuala Lumpur. Bernard Chandran's multicultural designs include Indian *saris*, Chinese-style sheath dresses, funky miniskirts, and wedding dresses. Best known for his lavish beadwork and embroidery, Chandran has become famous around the world. Bill Keith, one of the country's most respected designers, takes a different approach. He runs competitions to promote the traditional, figure-hugging *kebaya*. Entries include punk, grunge, and mini *kebayas*!

Fashion by internationally renowned designer Bernard Chandran is famous for its lavish trims.

15

FOOD

The great variety of food available in Malaysia reflects the different **ethnic groups** that have settled there, including Malays, Indians, Chinese, and Peranakan, or *Nonyas*. Herbs and spices from the nearby "spice islands" of Indonesia add zest to the fresh seafood, meat, fruit, and vegetables available locally.

Malay Food

Malay cooking is known for its rich, spicy flavors. These include garlic, ginger, chili, onions, turmeric, cumin, lemon grass, and nutmeg, together with a strong, tangy shrimp paste called *sambal*. Fresh seafood, beef, and chicken are popular. Any meat eaten by **Muslims** must be *halal*, which means that the animal has been killed by a special method. Pork is not eaten by Muslim Malays because their religion forbids it.

Ingredients are often stir-fried in oil with spices and herbs, then mixed with vegetables. Every meal is served with rice. Famous Malay dishes include satay, or morsels of meat threaded onto a skewer and barbecued, then dipped in peanut sauce. *Nasi lemak*, a popular breakfast dish, consists of sticky rice cooked in coconut milk and served with anchovies, *sambal*, boiled eggs, and cucumbers. On special occasions, *roti jala*—a type of pancakes—are made from flour, eggs, and herbs and served with a spicy sauce.

Nasi lemak is a simple meal of rice cooked in coconut milk, served with anchovies, cucumber, and chili gravy.

Indian Cuisine

Most of the Indians in Malaysia are Tamils from South India, who are mostly vegetarian. Hot, spicy vegetarian curries served with rice are popular. Curry puffs are delicious spicy vegetables wrapped in a puff pastry. At "banana-leaf restaurants" food is served on a fresh banana leaf and eaten with the fingers. When guests are full, they fold the leaf in half to indicate they have finished.

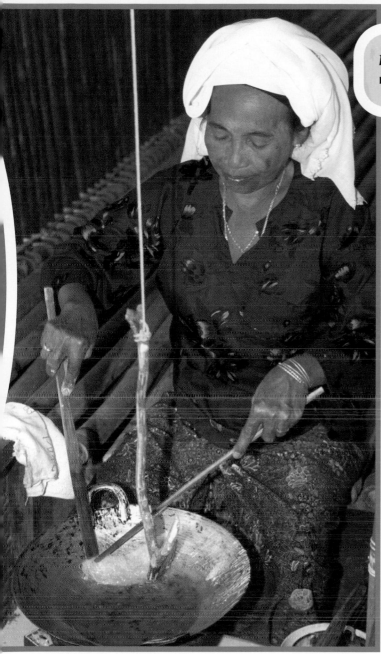

Chinese Cooking

Subtle flavors, fresh ingredients, and a huge variety of meats and vegetables are the key elements in Malaysian Chinese cooking. The meat is steamed or lightly stir-fried with plenty of vegetables. Popular dishes are the delicious *dim sum*—tasty steamed or fried morsels of food served in bamboo steamers—and chicken rice. The chicken is flavored with garlic, chili sauce, cucumbers, and coriander and served with rice.

Nonya Food

Home cooking is very important in *Nonya* culture, which mixes Chinese and Malay tastes. *Nonya* dishes are very complex and often take hours to prepare. Rich flavors of coconut milk, ginger, shallots, chilies, and carefully blended spices make the food famously tasty. Popular dishes include *popiah,* which is shredded vegetables in rolled-up pancakes, and sticky cakes made from sweet potatoes, sticky rice, sugar, and coconut milk.

Ice Cream in a Toilet

The large, green durian fruit has a hard spiny skin and soft white flesh. It is famous for its horrible smell and wonderful, sweet taste. Indeed, the Malays say it is "like eating ice cream in a toilet!" Its smell is so bad that the durian is banned from public buildings, airports, and many upscale hotels. Other tropical fruits include the huge jackfruit called *nangka,* with its mildly sweet flesh, and the mangosteen, with its juicy white pulp.

PERFORMING ARTS

Since ancient times, tribal people in Malaysia have celebrated with songs, dancing, and music. During religious **rituals,** shamans, or priests, were thought to be able to communicate with the spirit world through **trancelike** singing and dancing. Today, traditional forms of dance, music, and entertainment exist alongside a thriving modern performing arts scene. Western music is common in Malaysia's upbeat cities. Opera and classical orchestra concerts are well attended, and pop and rock have a huge following among young people. Theater companies explore current social and political issues, and ballet and modern dance are also popular.

Dance

The Kenyah people of Sarawak still perform the *datun julud* dance in honor of the **sacred** hornbill bird. This thanksgiving dance is performed by women in colored costumes, carrying fans made of hornbill feathers. Their headdresses are trimmed with goat hair tufts to mimic the images of their *bali,* or spirits. They are accompanied by men playing the *sape*, a stringed guitar carved from a single tree and painted with **intricate** patterns.

The national dance of Sabah is the *sumazau* of the Kadazan people. Two rows of men and women in traditional dress face each other, stretching their arms out in slow, flexible movements that resemble birds in flight. Gongs or drums accompany the dance.

A woman of the Kenyah people of Sarawak performs the *datun julud* dance in honor of the sacred hornbill bird.

The candle dance requires great skill to keep the flames upright as the dancers move around.

Ethnic Dances

The *joget* was introduced to the Malays by the Portuguese in the 1500s. Couples dance using rapid arm and foot movements to the lively beat of a flute, violin, and drums. The *joget* is often danced at weddings and is very popular.

The lovely candle dance called *tarian lilin* came to the Malaysian Peninsula from Sumatra with the Minangkabau people. Women hold lit candles on plates and make graceful, quick arm and hand movements, without toppling the candles or blowing them out. The lavish costumes worn by the performers include gold-trimmed sashes, long skirts, and the distinctive Minangkabau two-horned headpiece.

The *mak yong* is an ancient Malay dance-drama from Kelantan combining formal movements, acting, singing, words, and music. Originally forming part of spirit rituals, *mak yong* is traditionally performed by women who play heroes, clowns, gods, goddesses, spirits, and animals.

Ramli Ibrahim—Dance Guru

Ramli Ibrahim is one of the world's great classical dancers and teachers. He studied classical and modern ballet in Australia but soon turned to traditional Indian dance. At his Kuala Lumpur–based company, the Sutra Dance Theater, performances blend Indian dance styles with modern interpretations to produce highly original works that have won international fame.

Music

Traditional Malay music is based on percussion instruments, which are drums and gongs; wind instruments, which are nose and mouth flutes and bamboo pipes; and stringed instruments. The famous *gamelan* orchestra is made up of traditional gongs, drums, and xylophones. The *nafiri,* a large trumpet, and the *gambus*, a twelve-stringed lute, were brought to Malaysia by Arab traders centuries ago. Even more ancient are the *rebana ubi* drums of Kelantan near the border with Thailand. These large, wooden, cone-shaped drums were originally made from hollowed trees and used in village drum competitions in the celebrations after the rice harvest.

This is the cover of KRU's 2004 CD *Relax*.

Today's Music Scene

Devoutly Muslim Malaysia officially disapproves of Western-style pop stars. In 2003, Spice Girl look-alike group Elite caused an uproar when the group appeared on stage in unsuitable attire. But such disapproval does not stop young people from filling dance clubs and seeking out CDs by local bands like New Boyz or the former beauty queen turned pop star, Erra Fazira. The more casual approach of Indian and Chinese Malaysians to Western pop culture also fuels the modern music scene.

Rapsters

Three brothers make up the hugely successful rap group KRU. Their debut CD *Canggih* (1992) overturned the popular soft-pop ballad style to bring edgy rap to Malaysia. Although seven of the ten tracks were banned for "abusing the Malay language," the CD sold 65,000 copies. KRU caused another sensation in 1997 by recording a "duet" with long-dead music legend, P. Ramlee, by **dubbing** over his tracks. With a host of awards behind them, ten CDs, two films, and an international following, KRU is Malaysia's top group.

The *wayang kulit* shadow puppet theater is held outdoors at night and is accompanied by a traditional *gamelan* orchestra.

Theater

Shadow Puppets

Shadow puppet plays called *wayang kulit* were brought to Malaysia from Java in the 1200s and quickly became popular entertainment in the *kampung,* or villages. The puppets are made of flat buffalo hide and are finely cut out for showing in **silhouette.** The puppeteer sits behind a backlit screen, working the figures with rods from below. The puppeteer also directs the music and chants all the characters' voices. Stories are adventures from the great **Hindu** epic, the *Ramayana,* which features kings and princesses, evil demons, and the mischievous monkey-god, Hanuman. Music is provided by a *gamelan* orchestra.

Modern Theater

The Instant Café Theater in Kuala Lumpur is run by actor-director Jo Kukathas. It was established by her in 1989 as an **alternative theater** to present social and political comedy. Kukathas highlights human rights and the importance of free speech in her plays and is proud of the fact that her works have never been **censored** by the government.

The Actors Studio was set up in the same year by a husband–and–wife team, Joe Hasham and Faridah Merican. It has become one of Malaysia's best-known theater companies, training actors and theater technicians at its drama school, and presenting challenging plays in Tamil, *Bahasa Malaysia*, Chinese, and English to enthusiastic audiences. The Dan Dan Theater and Need Entertainment are two new companies that want to attract young Chinese actors to Malaysian theater with modern, topical works that push boundaries.

21

FOLKLORE
and Literature

Until the 1800s, few people in Malaysia could read or write. Stories, legends, and poems were learned by heart and passed down from one generation to the next. As schooling became more widespread, authors began to use the spoken, or common Malay language, and books became more popular. Today's writers explore many aspects of Malaysian culture, but the old legends and fairy tales have not died out.

Folk Tales

Long before ordinary people had access to books, folktales were told in the villages to entertain the community. These ancient tales are just as popular today.

Mousedeer and Crocodile

Almost every child in Malaysia knows the adventures of the mousedeer called Sang Kancil and its enemy, the big, bad crocodile Sang Buaya. In these stories, the mousedeer outsmarts the dimwitted crocodile, who never manages to capture the mousedeer. In one story, the mousedeer tricks the crocodile and a few of its friends into lining up across the river so the mousedeer can use them as stepping stones to reach some fruit on the other side.

The clever mousedeer always manages to outsmart its enemy, the crocodile Sang Buaya, in these famous folk tales.

Vampires

In Malaysian legends, vampires are particularly gruesome. Langsuyar began as a woman who died in childbirth. With her dead child, Pontianak, she roams about seeking victims and drinks their blood through a hole in her neck. She can be defeated by cutting off her long hair and nails.

The vampire Penanggalan is even more horrific. She takes the form of a flying head with **entrails** hanging from it, which work like octopus arms to capture victims. Thistles, or *jeruju,* keep this monster away and, according to legend, it is wise to hang them on doors and windows when a new baby is expected in the house.

Classic Works of Literature

Malaysia's greatest classic is *Sejarah Melayu: The Malay Annals* compiled by Tun Seri Lanang in 1536. Written in the classical Malay language, it charts the lives of the sultans of Melaka over 600 years, describing life at the royal court, heroic deeds, and important historical events.

The first writer to use the common Malay language was Munshi Abdullah Abdul Kadir (1796–1854). He is known as the father of Malaysian journalism for his lively, witty, and realistic writings about everyday life. These include his famous autobiography, *Hikayat Abdullah* (1843).

Leading Woman Writer

Shirley Geok-lin Lim, also known as Shirley Lim, was born in 1944 in Melaka and started writing when she was nine years old. Her 1996 **memoir** titled *Among the White Moon Faces* describes her struggle out of rural poverty and **discrimination** to become a writer and teacher in the United States. Lim's poetry collection, *Crossing the Peninsula*, won the Commonwealth Poetry Prize in 1980. She was both the first woman and the first Asian to receive this award.

Shirley Lim's novels and poems have gained her international fame.

Lat the Cartoonist

Newspapers around the world carry the comic strip Kampung Boy, or *Budak Kampung*, by famous cartoonist, Lat, whose real name is Mohammad Nor bin Khalid. His good-humored cartoons of a boy, Mat, and his village are based on Lat's home city of Ipoh, north of Kuala Lumpur. A thirteen-part animated series titled *Kampung Boy* was made by Lat in the United States in 1996 and screened around the world.

FILM
and Television

Malaysians are avid moviegoers, and almost everyone has access to television. In fact, some critics are worried that traditional entertainments like the *wayang kulit* puppet theater will die out because young people prefer films and television.

Early Films

The first film shot in Malaysia was *Laila Majnun* (1933), by Indian director B. S. Rajhans. He based his story on a traditional Malay opera and used opera singers as actors. The famous Chinese film producers, the Shaw brothers, made successful movies in the 1930s and 1940s, but the golden era of Malaysian film was the 1950s, with the rise of cinema legend, P. Ramlee (1929–1973).

Father of Malaysian Movies

P. Ramlee was first discovered by director B. S. Rajhans singing in a nightclub. Ramlee shot to fame with his first film *Cinta* (*Love*) in 1948 and starred in a further 63 films over 25 years. In 1957, he won Best Actor at the Asian Film Festival for his dual roles as father and son in the musical melodrama *Anakku Sazali—My Son, Sazali*. He began directing with the 1955 box office hit *Penarik Beca: The Trishaw Puller* and went on to direct 32 films, many of which became classics. Ramlee's dramatic acting and singing style helped shape the Malaysian film industry, and the music he composed and performed is still popular.

Legendary film actor, director, cameraperson, and singer-songwriter P. Ramlee was largely responsible for Malaysia's golden age of cinema in the 1950s and 1960s.

Movies Today

Local movies could not compete with television when it arrived in 1963. Hollywood dramas and imported Asian-action films have dominated theaters in Malaysia ever since. Despite government encouragement, only about fifteen Malaysian films are made a year. Some claim that strict **censorship** rules banning violence and love scenes discourage local filmmakers.

Art film director U-wei Hajisaari (1954–) got in trouble with the government with his controversial feature *The Arsonist* (1995). Although the film was selected for showing at the famous Cannes Film Festival in France—the only Malaysian film ever to be honored in this way—it was banned in Malaysia until 2001.

Many Malaysian films feature unrealistic plots that blend music, comedy, and drama. Kung-fu films are also popular. Local films have produced some fine actors, including the versatile veteran Mano Maniam, who writes, directs, and acts in film, television, and theater. In 1999, he appeared in the Hollywood film *Anna and the King*.

Television

Disney animations, lifestyle shows, and sitcoms are extremely popular with Malaysian viewers. Locally made comedy *Kopitiam (Coffee Shop)* was a smash hit. It centered on a group of misfits who hang out at a coffee shop and starred internationally acclaimed actors Joanna Bessey and Mano Maniam. *3R* is an edgy current affairs show for women. In 2003 it was banned for immorality when it interviewed two gay people. One of the producers who spoke out against the ban was former prime minister Dr. Mahathir Mohamad's daughter.

ARTS AND CRAFTS

Indigenous people in Malaysia have created art for centuries. The **gables** on longhouses were carved to welcome good spirits, boat prows were decorated to ensure safe journeys, and masks were made for religious **rites.** Later, **Islamic** art was expressed in the architecture and wall patterns of **mosques**. The Chinese, Indians, and English introduced painting and sculpture. Today, a wide variety of arts and crafts are produced in Malaysia, from traditional works to **abstract** sculptures.

Indigenous Art

In Sarawak, the Kenya and Kayan tribes carve elaborate wooden burial poles called *kelirieng* to guard the remains of village chiefs. Generally made from a single tree trunk up to 33 feet (10 meters) tall, *kelirieng* are hollowed out to hold the chief's bones as well as those of his followers and are topped with a huge stone slab.

The hornbill bird, with its curved beak and red crest, is **sacred** to the Iban of Sarawak. Hornbill statues, or *kenyalang,* are carved from wood, brilliantly decorated and surrounded by wooden human and animal figures.

This *kelirieng,* or burial pole, contains the remains of a Kajan princess who was the bride of a Kayan chieftain.

Tattoo Artists

Fine lines tattooed on an Iban warrior's hand once indicated that he had captured an enemy's head. While the Iban of Sarawak are no longer headhunters, they still practice tattooing. A sharp comb made of thorns is hammered into the flesh with a wooden mallet to create the design. The dye is made of soot mixed with pig fat or sugar syrup.

Fine Art

Fine art began around 1920 when a group of women, under the direction of famous Malay artist Abdullah Ariff, formed a group called the Penang Impressionists. These early artists were strongly influenced by European painting styles. Yong Mun Sen (1896–1962) was famous for his beautiful watercolor paintings. Trained in Chinese brush painting techniques, he produced light-filled, peaceful country scenes and seascapes. He helped set up the Penang Chinese Art Club in 1936 and is known as the "Father of Malaysian Painting."

Modern Master

Ibrahim Hussein (1936–) was born to poor parents in Kedah, but his talents won him opportunities to study in London and New York City. Hussein's works are semiabstract and often feature human figures, as well as brilliant colors and textures. He developed a technique he calls "printage," which combines printing and collage. His interest in current events almost landed him in prison in 1969 for **defacing** the Malaysian flag in his painting *May 13th*. Hussein's paintings are internationally acclaimed, and he has won dozens of awards.

Art Today

The government's National Culture Policy of 1971 promotes Islamic and Malay values in all artworks. Redza Piyadasa (1939–) is a lecturer, critic, and artist who supports the policy. His early sculptures and paintings followed modern Western styles, and his **installation** *A Matter of Time* (1978) featured a wooden kitchen chair with half the seat sawed out. Piyadasa's recent works, however, show strong local features, including photos of families in traditional costume. Despite the National Culture Policy, many young artists continue to push the boundaries, creating confronting installations and developing new directions in Web-based art.

Internationally acclaimed artist Charles Cham divides his time between Melaka and New York City. His works feature dark masks and figures on brightly colored backgrounds.

Traditional Handcrafts

A great variety of traditional handcrafts are made in Malaysia, including textiles, rattan, metalwork, and kites.

Textiles

Batik originated in Indonesia, but many claim Malaysian *batik* is the world's best. Cotton or silk cloth is patterned with melted wax, then dyed. The cloth is boiled to melt the wax, then repatterned, and redyed to produce complex designs. Patterns can be hand drawn in wax, stamped on with wooden blocks, screen-printed or tie-dyed.

Malaysian *batik* is known for its bright colors. It takes many applications of wax designs to produce the finished cloth.

Richly decorated fabrics are handwoven in Kelantan and Terengganu, where cloth called *kain songket* is made. The fabric is interwoven with gold and silver threads, which contrast with the bright colors in the weave.

Rattan Weaving

Rattan is made by weaving reeds into strong, dense mats. These lightweight, tough panels are used for house walls, sleeping mats, and baskets for storing food. In Sabah and Sarawak, leaves of the sago palm tree are stripped, dyed, and woven into intricate designs to make belts, jewelry, baskets, hats, and mats.

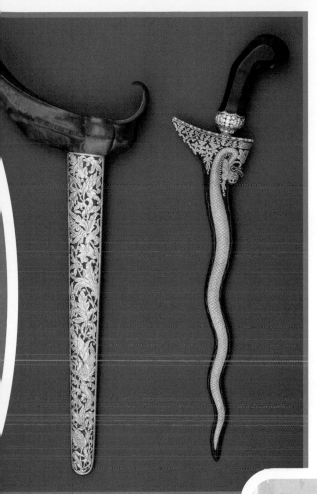

The *Kris* Dagger

Mystery and **ritual** surround the making of the famous wavy-bladed *kris* knife. The maker called *empu* is said to have magical powers. He fasts and prays and asks blessing from the *demit,* or good spirit, before beginning his work. The dagger is made from steel and a special iron made from **meteorites.** This gives the blade a pearly shine called the *pamor.* Layers of metal are beaten and folded many times, and teeth are etched into the blade. The dagger is then heated red hot and plunged into coconut oil. A *kris* is regarded as a **sacred** weapon. Offerings must be made to the spirit of the dagger, which is said to give special fighting powers to its owner, who can kill just by pointing the blade at the victim. Traditionally, the *kris* was an effective fighting weapon but today is used only for ceremonial purposes.

The *kris* dagger is regarded as a sacred object. The owner must respect the spirit of the dagger and make prayers and offerings to it.

Pewter

Pewter is a metal made of tin, **antimony,** and copper. Malaysia has the world's largest tin reserves and is famous for its fine pewter. The Royal Selangor Pewter Factory near Kuala Lumpur was founded in 1885 by Yoon Koon. It is still owned by his family. The soft gray sheen of the metal is shown at its best in the mugs, trays, statues, and bowls made by master craftspeople.

A Proud Achievement

Malaysia has a rich heritage in arts and crafts, dance, drama, and literature. Since **independence** in 1957, the government has been able to promote Malay culture without stifling the traditions and customs of the many other ethnic, racial, and religious groups who live there. The country stands as an example of how very different cultures can thrive side-by-side.

Flying High

Once, only the nobles of the ancient Melakan court could enjoy kite flying. Today, traditional kites called *wau* are made all over Malaysia. The bright colors are produced by pasting and layering cut-out paper designs on a bamboo frame. Tassels are added for decoration, plus a whistle that sings in the wind. Not just for show, these kites fly like birds.

GLOSSARY

abstract not realistic or not easy to understand

alternative theater nontraditional theater that presents new and challenging ideas

ancestor person from whom one is descended

animism religion in which followers believe that all things in the universe, living and nonliving, have a soul or spirit, and believe that spirits inhabit the natural world in places like mountains, rivers, and forests

antimony bluish-white metal

batik decorative fabric created by painting patterns onto cloth with melted wax, dying the cloth, then removing the wax

Buddhism religion in which followers study the teachings of the Buddha and strive for a peaceful state called enlightenment. A follower of Buddhism is a Buddhist.

censorship practice of preventing certain ideas or information from being freely communicated to the public

Christianity religion based on the belief in one God and the teachings of Jesus, as written in a holy book called the Bible. A follower of Christianity is called a Christian.

communal belonging to all members of a community

constitution set of written rules by which a country is governed

corruption dishonesty or criminal behavior for personal gain, especially in reference to government officials or other powerful people

deface spoil the image

designate specify; describe

devotion prayer and worship

devout sincerely religious

discriminate treat people unfairly on the basis of their race, gender, or religion, or for some other reason

diverse various kinds or forms

dub record over an existing soundtrack

entrails guts

ethnic group people who share a specific culture, language, and background

federal number of states forming one nation

gable triangular-shaped part of a wall under a roof-end

Hinduism diverse religion that originated in India; followers worship many gods and goddesses and believe in the rebirth of souls into new bodies after death. A follower of Hinduism is a Hindu.

immodest not modest; outrageous

independent free from foreign rule

indigenous original or native to a particular country or area

installation objects displayed as art

intricate finely worked; complicated

Islam Muslim religion, based on the teachings of the prophet Muhammad

lunar (calendar) measured by the phases of the moon

memoir memories that have been written down

meteorite rock that has fallen from outer space

monarchy government or country ruled by a hereditary leader such as a king or queen, often with limited powers

mosque building in which Muslims worship

multicultural made up of several different races or cultures

Muslim having to do with or following Islam, a religion based on belief in one god, called Allah. Muslims follow the teachings of the prophet Muhammad, as written in a holy book called the Qu'ran.

nomad person who roams from place to place without ever settling, usually following seasonal food supplies for flocks or herds

pilgrimage journey to a holy place

plantation large farm planted with crops

racial tension unrest between different races

rattan material made from woven reeds

reincarnation belief that humans are reborn after death

rite religious action or ceremony

ritual traditional religious or spiritual ceremony

sacred holy or religious

sacrifice offering to a god or goddess

salvation being saved

shantytown roughly built houses of the poor

silhouette black shape lit from behind

Syariah Law law that applies to Shi'ah Muslims

tolerance acceptance of differences

trance dreamlike state

INDEX

A

adat (Malay traditional law) 8

animism 7, 12

art 26–27

B

Bahasa Malaysia 6, 21

batik 15, 28

Borneo 4, 5, 12

Buddhism 7, 8, 9

C

censorship 5, 21, 25

Chinese New Year 9

Christianity 7

costume 14–15

crafts 28–29

D

dance 18–19

E

education 8, 12, 22

ethnic groups 4, 5, 6–7, 12–13

F

fashion 15

festivals 8–9, 10–11

film 24–25

flag 4

folktales 22

food 16–17

G

gamelan orchestra 20, 21

H

Hajisaari, U-wei 25

Hinduism 7, 8, 10, 16, 21

hornbill bird 11, 12, 18, 26

I

indigenous peoples 6–7, 8, 12–13, 14

Islam 7, 8

K

kebaya 15

Kelantan 7, 19, 28

kites 29

kris dagger 29

Kuala Lumpur 4, 5, 15, 19, 21

M

Malays 4, 6, 7, 8, 12, 13, 16, 19

music 20

N

national holidays 11

O

Orang Asli 4, 6, 7, 8, 12–13, 14

P

painting 26

Peranakans/Straits Chinese 6, 7, 16

pewter 29

puppetry 21

R

Rajhans, B. S. 24

Ramadan 7, 8

Ramlee, P. 20, 24

religions 7

S

Sabah 4, 5, 6, 12, 13, 14, 18, 28

Sarawak 4, 5, 6, 12, 14, 18, 26, 28

shadow puppet plays 21

shamans 18

T

tattoos 26

television 25

textiles 28

theater 21